the Polytunnel

# Companion

First published 2004

ISBN 09542555-77

A catalogue record for this book is available from the British Library.

**Published by**
Farming Books and Videos ltd.
PO Box 536
Preston
PR2 9ZY
www.farmingbooksandvideos.com

**Book designed and set by**
Surface
T. 01702 232058
E.surface99@btinternet.com

**Printed and bound in Great Britain by**
Bath Press

# the Polytunnel
# Companion

The Complete Guide
to Choosing and Using
your Polytunnel

by

Jayne Neville

BASIC GUIDES

## Acknowledgements

I would like to express my thanks to the following for their help in providing the answers to countless questions during the process of writing this book; Sean Barker of First Tunnels, Hugh Bryant-Evans of Ferryman Polytunnels, Richard Henbest of Visqueen, Howard Gawler of Gawler Plastics, David Nieburg and Jo Taylor of Country Herbs and Plants, Hugh Dorrington of Aveland Trees, and smallholders Piers Warren and Gary Beaman.

Last but not least, thanks to my husband, John Neville, for proof-reading the final manuscript, providing useful criticism and suggestions and for erecting the polytunnel that started it all ...

# Contents

Acknowledgements

Foreword

Chapter 1:      The Versatile Polytunnel.

Chapter 2:      Why Choose a Polytunnel?

Chapter 3:      Choosing Your Polytunnel.

Chapter 4:      A Suitable Site.

Chapter 5:      Polytunnel Accessories and Extras.

Chapter 6:      Putting it all Together.

Chapter 7:      Getting Ready for Growing.

Chapter 8:      Under Cover through the Seasons.

Chapter 9:      Pest Control.

Chapter 10:     Polytunnels Work for Them!

The Polytunnel Companion Checklists

Further Reading

Polytunnel Manufacturers and Accessories

Polythene Manufacturers

Seeds and Sundries

Hedging Suppliers

Organic Organisations

Index

# Foreword

This is the kind of book I wish I'd had to hand when I was thinking of buying my first polytunnel. When I first moved to my smallholding, sorting out somewhere for seed sowing, propagation and cultivating plants under cover was a real priority.

Because I'd previously owned a greenhouse, I knew how useful that had been – unfortunately I also knew that something on the scale I had in mind would be well beyond my budget, and so started thinking about acquiring a polytunnel. It was a struggle to find out much about them. The only literature readily available was from the polytunnel manufacturers themselves, some of it was most helpful, but what I really wanted was unbiased information from people who used polytunnels themselves.

I was also amazed to find out how infrequently polytunnels are featured in gardening books; sometimes just the merest of mentions, but most often ignored completely. Perhaps this is because they are still viewed as a more specialised form of crop protection and therefore only suitable for real enthusiasts and commercial growers. The main reason, though, I believe is through lack of information and understanding because many gardening writers do not have any experience of using polytunnels.

There is also still an undercurrent of prejudice that a polytunnel is simply a poor relation of the glasshouse: cheaper, less durable and uglier. This is a pity as growing under polythene can offer just as many rewards in the way of successful crops as a greenhouse – and in a big tunnel, more of them! They cost a lot less, their metal frames will last indefinitely and they are certainly no less attractive than an aluminium greenhouse!

As 'the new kid on the block' the polytunnel has proved itself on the very largest of scales, with commercial growers now using them as a first option, now it has to convince smaller operations such as smallholders and gardeners.

I hope this book will help to answer some of the questions would-be tunnel owners may have as well as providing useful hints and tips for more seasoned users. I've certainly never for a moment regretted my decision to go and buy one. I simply couldn't do without my polytunnel!

Jayne Neville

September 2003

(Editorial note. Throughout the text, when referring to polytunnel sizes, you will notice the emphasis is placed on Imperial measurements, followed by the metric equivalent. There is a reason for this - polytunnels sizes are more often referred to in feet and inches, the manufacturers commonly using Imperial measurements in their catalogues).

# Chapter 1

The Vine House at Audley End House in Essex, built in 1810, is a forerunner of the polytunnel making possible the cultivation of tender plants on a large scale in the unpredictable British climate.

# The Versatile Polytunnel

'... let me assure you that a polytunnel is a great thing to have...'
Hugh Fearnley-Whittingstall, River Cottage Cookbook.

Since its introduction in the late 1960s the polytunnel has become an increasingly popular choice for all types of grower, particularly over the last two decades. In the past, glasshouses were the only option available, but the invention of polythene has introduced a much cheaper alternative to those expensive glass structures – the polytunnel.

Prior to this, protected cultivation was invariably carried out in glasshouses; on a large scale in Victorian times within the walled kitchen gardens of many big country houses. A revival of interest in the history of gardening has ensured that many walled gardens have been restored along with the glasshouses contained in them.

One of the earliest and largest surviving examples is the glasshouse at Audley End House in Essex. Built in 1810, 'The Vinehouse', still houses a 200 year old grapevine and is also used to grow aubergines, tomatoes, peppers and ornamental plants.

Perhaps the grandest Victorian glasshouse of all, The Palm House, still stands in Kew Gardens in London. Arguably the world's most important surviving glass and iron structure, it took four years to construct and was specifically built to house a collection of exotic palms.

These early examples, although extravagant in both cost and size, were the forerunners of the polytunnel, and, for the first time made it possible to cultivate tender and more demanding plants on a larger scale in the unpredictable British climate.

Nowadays more modest sized glass greenhouses are still very popular, being used by the leisure gardener through to the large commercial nursery, but with the introduction of polythene covers, there is now an alternative. The choice between the aesthetic appeal of a glass structure compared to the simpler but perhaps less visually attractive combination of a polythene and steel one really depends on the individual and their situation.

A standard 14' x 25' polytunnel.

Polytunnels are far more versatile than traditional greenhouses. Here the owner has replaced the polythene for mesh.

## Top Tips

■ Remember to check out the manufacturers guarantee covering the polythene.

In a garden setting, a traditional wooden greenhouse is indeed more pleasing to the eye. But for sheer versatility and cost effectiveness, the polytunnel wins hands down. Simply put, a polytunnel is the cheapest way to get the largest protected area for cultivation. Many growers choose to use both glass and polythene - and why not? They each have their strengths and weaknesses as we will see later.

Tunnels come in all sizes, from the small – on a par with the average size garden greenhouse, to the very large – for commercial users. As well as for being used to grow fruit, vegetables and flowers, many tunnels house swimming pools, shelter animals or are used for storage.

One big concern for a first-time polytunnel owner is, will a polytunnel withstand extreme weather conditions? The vast number of commercial polytunnels now in use is a confirmation of their durability. In really windy areas, spacing the hoops closer together will ensure extra stability. Alternatively, many suppliers offer tunnels especially designed for exposed and windy sites.

In recent years improvements in the development of polythene has meant that now the polytunnel covers last much longer. Most manufacturers guarantee their polythene for four or five years, but many users report up to seven years or more before replacement is required.

For both smallholders and gardeners, polytunnels offer the chance to grow a wider variety of crops than they would outside and with careful planning, all year round. The variety of covers to choose from, i.e. thermal, mesh, UV, or partial polythene and mesh, mean that the tunnel can be used for other things throughout its life as the grower's situation changes. The frame can also be moved to a new area if required and further hoops added to increase the length if extra space is needed later. Internal partitions can be fitted inside; so if you are looking to heat just a section of your polytunnel, say for propagation purposes, it is easy to add an internal polythene divider and door.

Versatile, practical, cost effective and - just as important - somewhere to garden in comfort whatever the weather.

Welcome to the world of the polytunnel!

NOTES

# Chapter 2

## Why Choose a Polytunnel?

Both polytunnels and greenhouses are popular methods of achieving protected cultivation. The British climate offers a relatively short season for the cultivation of crops so anything which helps to prolong the growing period dramatically affects productivity. Having an area to grow in sheltered from the wind, rain and frost is a great advantage. A polytunnel or greenhouse extends the growing season at each end of the year so spring crops can be ready 6-8 weeks earlier than those grown outside and during the autumn and winter, fresh salads and vegetables are a welcome addition to the late season menu.

A polytunnel extends the growing season at each end of the year.

Once you own a polytunnel, you will be able to raise your own vegetables, summer bedding plants and flowers from seed, either with or without using heated propagation methods. Delicate and exotic plants, which would not survive outside such as melons, aubergines, cucumbers and peppers, can all be successfully grown. Tender plants can stay in the tunnel until all danger of frost is past. Hanging baskets can be planted up, and suspended in the tunnel, growing on until conditions are right and they can be placed outside.

Why then, would you choose a polytunnel instead of greenhouse?

Cost effectiveness is one major advantage. Even a relatively small greenhouse can be expensive. A polytunnel works out much cheaper and the larger the area it covers the relatively cheaper it becomes. Buy the biggest size you can afford, the extra space will be well worth the additional cost and I can guarantee you will always find something to fill it!

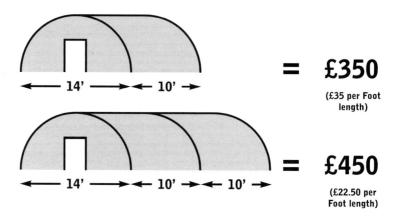

= **£350**

(£35 per Foot length)

= **£450**

(£22.50 per Foot length)

Polytunnels become relatively less expensive the larger they are.
(Example costs for illustrative purposes only).

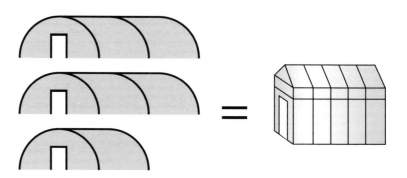

A 8' x 12' polytunnel is 2.5 times cheaper than a greenhouse of an equal size.
(Based on average prices).

A polytunnel is easier to construct than a greenhouse with generally far fewer pieces to put together.

A polytunnel is easier to construct. Generally there are far fewer pieces to have to put together compared with a greenhouse and a polytunnel has the advantage of being more easily moved should you decide at a later date that the current position is not ideal.

Traditionally, the control of heating and ventilation has always been better in a greenhouse and indeed glass does tend to retain heat within the structure better than polythene. It is also less likely to cause condensation, although the modern types of polythene are much improved in this respect. However, over the last few years, polytunnel manufacturers have increased the options available and are now able to offer tunnels with ventilation panels and thermal grade polythene offering better heat retention. Other 'extras' such as a choice of door designs, overhead crop bars for stability and suspending frames for climbing plants and hanging baskets and even custom made irrigation systems are now also readily available.

Polytunnels are more versatile. You have more choice over the material used to cover the structure. Most manufacturers supply their polytunnels in kit form and offer at least two different grades of polythene, standard and thermal/anti-fog. In the early days of the polytunnel, the traditional 'half-moon' shape was all that was available. This design is structurally very strong and the curved sides mean the structure is very stable under windy conditions. The only disadvantage of this is that plants inside cannot be grown too close to the edge of the tunnel due to the reduced height at the sides. Now tunnels can be obtained with vertical sides, enabling cultivation to take place right up to the edge of the polythene, with an available growing height similar to that offered by the straight sides of a greenhouse.

## Top Tips

■ Remember to buy the biggest size your budget will stretch to — you won't regret it.

■ Remember to include 'extras' such as doors, irrigation and crop bars in your budget.

The versatility of the polytunnel is demonstrated here with the owner creating an indoor swimming pool.

The polytunnels themselves can be used to provide protection for surrounding crops on the outside.

Polytunnels can adapt to suit the needs of the grower; they can be made larger by adding more hoops, given better ventilation, different covers, and can be relatively easy to move to a new site if required. How about using it as a giant fruit cage which can be easily achieved using netting ordered from the manufacturer in the same way as a replacement polythene cover? For the owner of livestock, it is a secure and dry place for animals during the worst of the winter, for example during lambing when it is an advantage to confine sheep so one can keep a close eye on them. Many polytunnels are successfully used by poultry breeders and can be adapted in a variety of ways to suit the needs of the young birds as they grow. For young chicks, an overhead brooder lamp can easily be suspended from the frame.

During wet periods in the summer or autumn, the inside of a polytunnel is a perfect spot for drying off vegetables such as onions and potatoes before storing them for later use. The central ridge pole is an ideal place to work from when you are stringing onions, and is also useful for tying up bunches of flowers for drying.

Larger width polytunnels can be used to cover swimming pools and as storage areas for farm and smallholding machinery such as tractors and other implements.

Polytunnels themselves can be used for outside crop protection. The space between two tunnels placed side by side can create a protected growing area for plants requiring a sheltered site outside. Posts supporting heavy gauge netting erected at each end will make sure the windbreak effect is complete on all sides.

# Chapter 3

## Choosing a Polytunnel

First of all, decide what you want from your polytunnel.

What do you want to grow and how much do you want to grow? Will the crops you cultivate be solely for your family's consumption or are you planning to grow your produce for sale to the public? Although it is fairly important that you make an initial choice that's right for your current needs, all will not be lost if you change your mind in years to come. A polytunnel can be adapted in many ways to suit the changing requirements of the grower.

Once you have established why you need a polytunnel, the next question is, how much can you afford to spend? It's a good idea to contact several different suppliers to compare prices and more importantly see what each one can offer. Some manufacturers can supply optional extras such as irrigation kits, fitted staging, ventilation sheets and much more. Never be afraid to ask for help and advice when you are choosing. Many of the concerns and queries you may have will have been voiced before by other would-be tunnel owners and can probably be answered quite simply.

A multispan tunnel is a single structure that looks like a lot of single tunnels joined together.

## Top Tips

■ Remember to check out with each supplier what is included in the price and what optional extras there are.

Let's take a look at the various styles of polytunnel available. There are two main types: single span and multi-span. The obvious difference between them apart from size is in the design. Multi-span tunnels look like two, three or more single polytunnels joined together, but are in fact one large single structure. They include rain gutters that can also be used for tensioning the polythene. Because of their sheer size and more complicated frame structure, multi-span tunnels are normally erected by specialist companies, and are therefore out of the scope of the DIYer. They are also, as one would expect, much more expensive to buy. Some polytunnel manufacturers are able to supply both types but others specialise in just one or the other. Smaller growers usually opt for single span tunnels, with larger scale enterprises choosing multi's.

Size-wise, single span polytunnels usually start from widths of 8 feet (2.44m) to up to 30 feet (9.14m). The length really depends on what you want as extra space is gained with every additional hoop added. As already mentioned, polytunnels are available with vertical sides that allow full use of the floor area as well as the more traditional shape.

Vertical sides allow full use of the floor area

Crop bars running along the top of the hoops introduce greater strength, useful in particularly windy areas.

Having evaluated your site and weather conditions, you should be able to choose the type of frame you need. If you live in a sheltered area you may find that one of the standard models will be adequate for your needs. Even the average frame can withstand high windspeeds – check with your supplier at the time you place your order. If a windbreak is erected around the structure, the strength of the wind will be effectively lessened anyway.

There are many tunnels specifically designed to take windy conditions in their stride. These structures usually have stronger, wider diameter hoops, and the manufacturer's instructions may well suggest that they are spaced slightly closer together than is the norm. Standard hoop spacing in a single span polytunnel is usually 6 – 8 feet apart; in a heavy-duty tunnel 5 feet apart is not unusual. For even more strength, an optional extra is an additional brace between each hoop or by the addition of 'crop bars' which run along the top of the hoops. As well as making the whole structure more secure the crop bars can be used to support frames for climbing plants and for somewhere to suspend hanging baskets early in the season. The cost of these tunnels is slightly more, but the expense is well worth the piece of mind and the effort of having to re-erect or recover a tunnel that has blown down in a gale! Strengthened tunnels have survived windspeeds of around 130 mph. And the fact that they are used in places like the Hebrides, Falkland and Orkney Islands bears testament to their tenacity!

The next question is what to cover it with. This is not quite as simple as it sounds as there are several different grades of polythene to choose from, not to mention other materials such as mesh for different growing applications. If you are buying a polytunnel kit from a supplier then they will probably have a choice of materials for you to choose from. These should be described in their brochure along with the attributes of each one.

Now is also the time to mention Anti Hot Spot tape. This is a self adhesive foam tape which is fixed onto the tunnel hoops before fitting the cover. The tape protects the polythene from the hot metal hoops during summer and stops the cover chafing. Check if this tape is included in the price of your polytunnel kit. Quite often, it has to be ordered separately, but as it can extend the life of your cover by at least one year, it is a wise investment.

The polythene used on polytunnels has improved drastically over the last few years, with even the cheapest options guaranteed for four years. Many users report their covers lasting as long as ten years. Here are the most likely grades you will encounter:

- Standard polythene (EVA/UVI 720 gauge).

This is the traditional clear tunnel polythene, ideal for the British climate where light levels are normally low and where the tunnel will be used to grow crops mainly during the warmer months. The film allows 95% light transmission which helps prevent plants competing with each other for light, ensuring strong healthy growth.
This cover is especially designed for use when growing frost hardy crops, which do not require any form of heat during the winter such as hardy perennials. As a place for production of summer vegetables or flowers, this material is more than adequate. The cover is guaranteed for four years.

## Top Tips

■ Remember to check if necessary items such as Anti-Hot Spot tape are included in the cost.

- Thermal/Anti Fog polythene (EVA/UVI 720 gauge + UVA and UVB filters).

As the name suggests, this is more heat retentive than standard polythene. Heat is trapped inside the tunnel for longer due to an infrared additive in the polythene. A polytunnel covered in thermal film can be as much as 2°C higher on a frosty night than the standard sheet. It will warm the tunnel up faster in the morning and cool down much more slowly at night. The ideal cover for heated polytunnels, it is possible to achieve a saving of between 15-20% on heating costs so it is ideal for over winter vegetable production and early sowing of annual plants.

The anti fogging agent helps to channel moisture and condensation down the sides of the tunnel, rather than dripping down onto the plants. This helps to reduce fungal diseases such as mildew and botrytis, both of which thrive in damp conditions. Good light transmission is also a feature of this film and it again carries a guarantee of four years.

- White/Super White (UVI)

This cover appears milky white rather than clear. The opaqueness of the film reduces light transmission to 70% which in turn affects the temperature inside the tunnel. The shading effect creates a cooler temperature and slightly diffused light which certain plants require. The risk of scorching is eradicated.

Super White is also suitable for using on tunnels used for storage, to house livestock or to cover swimming pools.

The introduction of an intermediate door is useful for dividing the tunnel into areas for different uses.

- Mesh/net/windbreak

The commonest mesh material used to cover tunnels is green net. Covering a tunnel in net is usually more expensive than using a polythene sheet, but has its advantages for protecting certain crops. Utilised as a fruit cage it will protect soft fruit from birds. There are various different types on the market, some of the smaller mesh net can even exclude some insects, although if used for fruit, don't forget that pollinating insects need to be able to gain access, or you won't get any fruit!

Used as a shade or windbreak material, mesh can protect specialist plants or ones that need a certain level of protection from extreme weather conditions.

- Other materials.

In the past, polythene covers have also been manufactured in translucent green and blue, but these have now fallen from grace. Originally intended to reduce sun scorch, the downside was that on cloudy days, the low light levels caused the plants inside the tunnel to 'stretch' giving weaker growth. Similar to the Super White, crops needing protection from the sun will thrive under this type of cover, but if growing a wide variety of plants, a clear cover is a safer bet.

### Doors and Ventilation

In many polytunnels, especially the smaller sizes, the doors at either end are the only means of ventilation. For most growing situations, this can be quite adequate as long as both doors are opened during warm conditions ensuring some movement of air. The simplest form of door is in the shape of a blind, which can be rolled up or down. An alternative is to fit a hinged door, which is basically a wooden frame covered with polythene. This door can either be wholly covered in polythene or the top half mesh with the lower half polythene.

Wider tunnels can be fitted with double doors - a good idea if you need to get machinery in and out or require better ventilation.

Side vents give more control over the polytunnel environment.

A more recent innovation is the use of an intermediate partition and door, which is very useful for dividing the tunnel into areas for different uses. Not all manufacturers offer this option so shop around if you feel this is an extra you would like.

Better ventilation can be achieved by the addition of a net skirt which replaces the polythene around the lower side sections of the tunnel. This is even better when used with a ventilation panel consisting of a polythene screen that can be raised or lowered to cover the mesh, giving the grower much more temperature control. The system is operated by means of a simple winding gear.

### A note about buying secondhand

You may come across secondhand tunnels for sale from time to time. These will probably be advertised locally, in the press or at farm auctions. Quite often the buyer will have to dismantle the polytunnel as well. This will be quite challenging if the foundation tubes have been cemented into the ground. If the polytunnel has been standing in situ for some time the hoops may well be quite tightly fixed. The good thing about dismantling yourself however is that you can see exactly what goes where and that you have all the fittings needed to put the polytunnel back up! Buying one already dismantled might mean some of the pieces are missing. Don't forget to budget for transport costs to get it home.

Obviously you will need to order new polythene to cover it as you cannot reuse the original one. Most tunnel manufacturers can supply polythene film only. Alternatively you can contact a specialist horticultural film supplier, who will be able to offer an even wider range of materials. If you are thinking of specialising in one or two particular crops, they will be able to advise the best cover for you.

Personally I have never bought a secondhand tunnel, but if you have an eye for a bargain and don't mind sourcing a new polythene cover and any missing fixtures and fittings, you will certainly pay a lot less for it than buying new.

NOTES

polytunnel must be sited on
el ground.

# A Suitable Site

Now you have chosen your tunnel where should you put it? Siting the polytunnel is of the utmost importance and there are many things to take into consideration, such as the ground level, light levels and exposure to the elements, especially wind, on the site you choose. If you live in an area particularly prone to extreme weather conditions, do not despair, there are measures you can take to make your site more polytunnel friendly. Polytunnels, especially heavy duty ones, can be situated in the most inhospitable settings.

If there are other polytunnels in your vicinity, take a careful note of where they have been sited. Have a word with other local tunnel owners, who will be able to give you an insight into the pitfalls which may occur if you do not take local factors into account. Many will have learned by their mistakes and will be more than happy to pass on their wisdom to you.

Have a chat with the Planning Officer at your local council's Planning Department. Smaller tunnels do not usually need planning permission, being classed along similar lines to greenhouses, but for larger structures permission will be needed and it is always best to check as planning rules and regulations are apt to change from time to time, and different areas vary.

Make sure your chosen site is as perfect as it can be by checking the following:

- Is the polytunnel site level and what is the condition of the soil (soft or clayey)? This will affect the method you use to anchor the foundation tubes into the soil. Many heavier soils will be able to hold the tubes securely without any need for cementing in, but lighter, sandier soil may need extra help by way of cement.

- Take into account the direction of the prevailing wind. If you are in a particularly exposed, wind prone area, it is wise to think about erecting a windbreak (see below).

## op Tips

Remember polytunnels
1 be situated in the most
ospitable settings.

- **Strategic positioning of your polytunnel can affect the temperature inside.** It is generally accepted that an orientation of north to south, will generate slightly lower temperatures during the day than east to west where the sun tracks across the long side of the tunnel. A cooler temperature is preferable as it reduces the risk of sun scorch and certain pest and disease problems.

- **If there are tall buildings or trees close to the site,** assess if they will cut down light in the tunnel. Large tree roots could also have an effect on the soil in the polytunnel if the trees are too close to it.

- **If you are intending using electricity** in the polytunnel for example for propagation, does the site lend itself to an electricity supply?

- **If needing access for machinery,** can you get to the polytunnel with reasonable ease, even in the winter when the ground will be wet and muddy?

- **Are there implications for irrigation?** What methods do you want to use? Will a simple watering can or a hose pipe suffice, or will you be using rainwater collected in a tank or water butt?

ke full use, if you can, of any natural
elter afforded by trees or hedges.

Windbreaks

Severe weather conditions, especially gales, are the most likely cause of damage to polytunnels. As the polythene ages, the more delicate it becomes and any extra protection you can give it by way of a windbreak will pay dividends – and peace of mind.

Take a look at what other polytunnel owners have done to protect their structures. Have they put them in amongst other buildings, behind a tree shelter belt or used purpose- made windbreaks to shelter them from the strongest winds? Even the remains of a damaged tunnel can give clues of where NOT to site one.

The easiest and cheapest option is if you already have a tall hedge growing on your land. Sited alongside, the polytunnel will benefit from the wind speed reducing effect the hedge has, without sacrificing any light reduction. This of course is if you are lucky enough to have a hedge in the right place! We have a double row of tall willows running along one of our boundaries. This hedge more or less protects the tunnel from the strong southerly winds. How fortunate that our predecessor planted them before he moved, several years ago!

**op Tips**

Remember to study what
her owners have done to
otect their structures from wind.

Willows are a good option for a shelter belt, being very fast growing (some varieties can reach up to 3 metres in the first year), and tolerant of even the most inhospitable situations. However, any kind of native hedge would be as good eventually, but will take several years to reach a useful height. If you decide to plant any kind of hedging as a windbreak don't forget to leave a wide gap between the hedge and the proposed polytunnel site. If planted too close, as well as cutting down on the light, roots from the hedge could eventually encroach on the soil in your tunnel. You will also need to leave some free space around the polytunnel to make access easier for you when the time comes for cleaning the polythene cover.

But what if you have no hedge, and no time to grow one? If you have outbuildings or even a glasshouse that can afford protection from the wind, could you put your tunnel alongside? This is exactly what many professional growers do.

The final option is to make a windbreak yourself. At least you can put it exactly where it is needed. This needs to be no more elaborate than several poles driven into the ground with windbreak netting drawn taut between them. Although perhaps too cumbersome to protect a smaller tunnel, the photo here shows telegraph poles being used to support windbreak material. This is a popular method of wind protection used by commercial enterprises in the Lincolnshire Fens, so it must work!

Telegraph poles can provide an adequate windbreak.

de or seep hose installed prior to planting work.

# Polytunnel Accessories and Extras

These are items that will help you customise your tunnel to suit your needs. Chosen carefully, these items will make your life, in terms of growing, that much easier. Just think of accessories as time management tools.

### Irrigation equipment

First of all, let us turn to that basic plant requirement – water. Without it, the protected climate on the inside of your polytunnel will quickly turn into a desert. During the winter, using a watering can or hand-held hose pipe once a week or even less, is an easy task, especially in a smaller size tunnel. When summer arrives, however, keeping it well watered is a major issue, and can become a burden unless other methods are employed.

From a simple trickle irrigation hose to overhead watering systems, your irrigation system can be as easy or sophisticated as you require.

- **Trickle or seep hose.** This consists of a porous pipe which is positioned around the plants on the polytunnel floor. Linked to a normal hose, the water seeps out into the surrounding soil.

- **Leaky pipe.** Similar to the above, but this is a normal hose pipe which has tiny holes along its length. It can be positioned around the plants so that the holes face upwards, giving a fine overhead spray of water, or with the holes facing down into the soil, which gives an effect similar to the trickle hose. Do check occasionally to make sure that the holes aren't blocked up.

Overhead irrigation kits are favoured by most commercial growers.

• **Overhead irrigation kits.** This is the method that most commercial growers favour, ensuring that crops get watered efficiently and with the minimum of effort. The system is most effective in the larger size tunnels (16' wide (4.88m) and over) where supplying water to the plants with a hose pipe would be extremely time consuming. Overhead watering can be supplied via one single pipe running along the length of the ridge pole, or for larger structures, a twin line system, with a pipe on either side of the ridge.

## Propagators

Whether or not you want to invest in a propagator is up to you and will probably be dictated by what it is you want to grow and when. If you are after earlier crops, then a propagator will get your plants off to a flying start, but be careful that your tunnel is adequately warm when the young plants are first taken out of the propagator. If it is still early in the season, a sudden change in temperature will severely check growth or even worse, kill the plant. Germination of most vegetable seeds happens when the soil temperature is between 12-16°C (55-68°F) depending on variety and is much more reliable when the source of the heat comes from underneath. You have probably heard the term 'bottom heat', and this is exactly what electric propagators provide.

Electric propagators will get your plants off to a flying start.

Electric, thermostatically controlled propagators are widely available, ranging in size and able to handle one, two or several standard seed trays at once. Some growers make up their own propagators using heat mats or panels.

If you have no electricity supply to your tunnel, all is not lost. Leaving your seed sowing until a few weeks later when the outside temperature is higher will not set you back too much in terms of time. Quite often, seeds sown without artificial heat are slightly more sturdy and will sometimes catch up with earlier, artificially heated ones. You can buy unheated propagators consisting of a polystyrene base and rigid clear plastic cover that are most effective. Even simpler is a standard seed tray and clear plastic lid with adjustable vents. Alternatively, you can cover a seed tray with a sheet of glass until the first shoots appear. A warm kitchen windowsill is as good a place as any, or a place in the airing cupboard – so long as you move them into the light as soon as germination is apparent.

Electric heaters come in a
wider choice of styles and are
thermostatically controlled.

## Heaters

If you wish to heat your polytunnel then you have a variety of heaters to choose from. Make sure you carefully calculate the internal area of your tunnel to ensure the heater you choose is powerful enough to cope. If part of the tunnel is sectioned off to create a separate germination and propagation area, then so much the better – the heat can be contained there and not spread around the rest of the polytunnel where it is not needed. A small area like this could also be insulated with bubble wrap material suitable for greenhouses, fixed to the frame using clips.

In larger structures a circulation fan can be used to improve the heat distribution. Suspended from the polytunnel ridge, a fan will also reduce condensation.

- **Paraffin heaters:** still the mainstay heater for amateur gardeners, these heaters come in various sizes. Although cheap to run, even the biggest size is not really powerful enough for many polytunnels, except as an anti-frost heater. They have no thermostats and stay on all the time.

- **Electric heaters:** these of course will only be an option if you have an electricity supply linked to your polytunnel. There is a lot more choice available and electric heaters are thermostatically controlled and simple to use. They are the most expensive heaters to run however and heater prices vary depending on design.

## Top Tips

■ Remember to calculate
the internal area of the
tunnel to ensure the heater
is powerful enough.

A gas heater offers the cheapest running costs but are most expensive to buy

Some staging kits are tailor made to be fixed to the tunnel frame.

- **Gas heaters:** a gas heater offers the cheapest running costs of all and provides a convenient method of heating the polytunnel. Thermostatically controlled, they are also the most expensive heaters to buy.

- **Heaters** for heating and frost prevention: there are some heaters specifically made for keeping the temperature at just above freezing. This is very useful if you overwinter plants in your polytunnel. These heaters are fitted with a frost stat which only comes into play when the air temperature drops towards freezing. An economical option as it operates only when needed.

### Staging

Some staging kits are tailor-made to be fixed to the tunnel frame. This is a simple but effective idea, and makes for a very sturdy workbench. Basically, the polytunnel hoops are used to hold up one side of the staging using clamps and brackets, the other side has legs as in conventional free-standing staging. A work top for potting, growing on, etc., is fitted onto the frame. This type of staging can run the whole length of the tunnel on both sides if required. The advantage of free-standing staging is that you can use either the sort manufactured for use in greenhouses, or make your own. Most garden centres and DIY stores stock staging usually in aluminium or wood. The staging can be placed wherever you want and can easily be moved to another position if required. The disadvantage is that unless you lay slabs on the ground where the staging is to stand, the staging supports will have a tendency to sink into the soil over time.

Making staging yourself is a simple DIY project and can of course be made up to whatever size you want. The supports can be made on a frame so that the staging stays on top of the soil, not in it!

## Thermometers

A thermometer is a must for any polytunnel. The most popular one used in greenhouses and polytunnels is the maximum-minimum thermometer, ideal for monitoring temperatures over 24 hours. These are usually reset by either pressing a button or using a magnet to draw the mercury down to the starting point.

Digital thermometers are very accurate, many of them quite sophisticated! As well as recording max-min temperatures some are equipped with a memory to record previous readings.

## Plant supports and frames

Perhaps not thought of until late spring and early summer, it certainly pays to ponder on the question of how you will support tall plants like tomatoes and cucumbers in advance. Even in the initial stages of choosing your tunnel, if you are planning to grow something that will need a frame or support, decide whether the optional extra of crop support bars might be worth the extra expense.

NOTES

# Chapter 6

## Putting it all Together

The day your new polytunnel arrives will be an exciting one! Don't be daunted by the array of components when you've unpacked them all. No doubt your kit will arrive with a set of instructions and the telephone help line number of the manufacturer who will give you guidance if you get stuck.

The pictorial guide in this chapter aims to show you the basics of how to erect a polytunnel in easy stages. Some tunnels will vary slightly from this, but the principles are the same. If you work methodically, using your manufacturer's instructions you won't find it too difficult. The length of time it takes to erect and clad a polytunnel depends on you — and how many helpers you have! The 14' x 25' tunnel in the photographs took two full days to complete and was erected by two people. It does pay to have more in the way of assistance when you fit the cover, especially if your tunnel is larger than this. It took us one day to erect the frame and doors, and one day to fix the anti-hot spot tape and fit and attach the polythene cover.

**Choose a fine, dry day if possible.** This will not only make the job a lot more comfortable for you, but a warm, calm day with little or no breeze is essential when fitting the polythene!

**Make sure you have everything to hand before you start.** Check that you have all the correct polytunnel pieces and have at hand all the tools needed for the job: hammer, tape measure, sledge hammer or mallet, scissors, spade, step ladder — there is nothing more annoying than having to hunt around for a missing tool when you are at a crucial point in the proceedings!

You will already have chosen a level site for your tunnel and cleared it of any debris and weeds. Begin to measure out exactly where the tunnel will go, accurately marking out the position of the foundation tubes which will hold the main tunnel frame into the ground. Check that the diagonals are equal to ensure your measurements are square.

Lay the foundation tubes in their exact positions before driving them into the soil. Some tunnels have closer hoop spacing than others – make sure you know whether yours is 5 feet, 6 feet or whatever. Depending on your soil type, you may need to cement the foundation tubes in position. Be careful when driving the tubes in not to damage them, or you may not be able to push the half hoops into them! Use a piece of wood as a buffer to eliminate this problem.

Step 1: Lay the foundation tubes in their exact positions before driving them into the soil.

Step 2: Drive the tubes into the soil using a wood buffer to prevent damage.

Step 3: Once the tubes are firmly in place push the half hoops into them.

Step 4: Connect the half hoops down the centre of the tunnel using the ridge connectors.

Step 5: Mark out and dig the trench around the frame.

Once the tubes are firmly in place push the half hoops into them. Sometimes the half hoops are manufactured with small holes in which to insert nails that hold the hoops in an exact position in the tubes. There are sometimes two sets of holes, so ensure you select the same set all the way around. The reason for the two holes is so that you can re-tension the polythene if needed in the future by raising the frame up to the higher hole.

Connect the half hoops down the centre of the tunnel using the ridge connectors. Now it's starting to look like a polytunnel.

Mark out and dig the trench around the frame, leaving a few inches clearance from the hoops (if you dig too close the soil surrounding the tunnel frame will start to collapse) This trench should measure 12" x 12" (30.5cm x 30.5cm). There is no need for it to go completely around the structure, leave the soil intact where the doorways are to be.

Base rails are an alternative to digging out a trench.

Fixing white foam tape – Anti Hot Spot tape – will prolong the life of the polytunnel.

## Top Tips

■ Remember to have all your tools ready before you start the construction.

There is an alternative method to burying the surplus polythene in a trench. This takes the form of fixing treated timber rails all around the base of the tunnel frame at almost ground level. Once the cover is over the polytunnel frame it is pulled down around the rails and fixed in place using battens. If this is a construction route you want to take, choose your manufacturer carefully, as not all supply this option.

If your kit comes complete with the timber for the doors, the frame will need to be fitted at this time. The doorframe is actually a very important part of your tunnel as it is this which will hold your polythene tight onto the frame. The uprights should be inserted into the ground at least 1 foot and firmly bedded in. Attach them to the top of the hoop by metal straps, folded around the hoop then nailed onto each side of the door upright. Fix the top horizontal of the doorway to the uprights.

An important part of erecting a polytunnel, at least in terms of prolonging the life of the cover, is affixing a white foam tape, known as Anti Hot Spot tape. This stops the polythene chafing against the metal, and will protect it from contact with the hot metal on scorching summer days. The tape is affixed to the outside edge of the frame where the polythene will come into contact with the metal. The tape is extremely sticky so try and fix it accurately first time as it is very difficult to remove and will get damaged in the process.

The completed polytunnel without the door.

...ting a door blind.

...e door catch.

Your frame is now complete and ready for cladding with polythene. Carefully unpack the polythene – it should come on a roll. If your kit has a closure; either a door blind or standard door, you may have to cut the polythene for this yourself from the main sheet. Ensure that this is the case or if the door polythene has been already cut for you.

The remainder of the polythene is for the tunnel itself. Start at one end, rolling the sheet right along the ridge to the other end. Check that the polythene is equal either side – our cover had a useful line of printing running along the middle so we knew we had it centrally positioned. Pull the polythene drum tight a section at a time, attaching it to the door frame as you go. This is when it is useful to have a few more pairs of hands, and a warm, calm day as this makes the cover more pliant. Adjustments can be made by re-tensioning the polythene on the door frame at this stage if it is found to be too slack. Some tunnel kits allow you to raise the hoops in the foundation tubes which also re-tensions the film, but it is better to get it right in these initial stages rather than taking remedial measures later on.

Your manufacturer's instructions should be followed with regard to making up the doors, as there are a variety of different styles. The one shown here is fitted with a door blind which is rolled up or down as required. The blind is held in place by simple wooden catches and can be fully or partially opened depending on the ventilation required.

## Top Tips

■ Remember the door frame is
...n essential part of the polytunnel.

■ Remember to ask the
...anufacturer if the polythene
...as guide lines to help you
...entralise it on the frame.

Slabs can be laid straight onto prepared level soil to create a path.

The final part of the operation is the making of a path down the centre, or slightly off centre, of the tunnel. This can be made of slabs, mulch, or whatever you like. The path should be wide enough to allow easy access for tools such as wheelbarrows or any machinery that you may wish to use in the polytunnel. The reason for choosing to lay a path off centre is a good choice if you are planning to use the central ridge pole for suspending hanging baskets or using it to support your climbing plants.

Slabs can be laid straight onto prepared level soil or you may wish to lay them on top of a weed suppressing material to prevent weed problems later. If you prefer to use mulch as your path, then some form of barrier should be used to contain it, otherwise the mulch will migrate fairly rapidly into the soil beds! The easiest barriers to erect are simply lengths of wood running along the edge of the path held in place by wooden pegs. These of course will deteriorate over time, but will effectively keep the path separate from the soil for several years. Alternatively, you could make raised beds on each side of the path from old railway sleepers; providing both a path and generous deep beds for your crops.

## Top Tips

■ Remember to lay paving slabs on Weed-Suppressing material to avoid weed problems later.

NOTES

The soil inside the polytunnel will be the same as outside so you should have an idea of how it will perform.

**Chapter 7**

# Getting Ready for Growing

Once your polytunnel is up, you'll want to start using it as soon as possible. However, time spent planning and preparing will play dividends in the long term, so don't rush into things too quickly!

First, let's turn to the basics: the soil. The soil in your polytunnel will be the same as the soil outside of course, and so you should have a good idea of how it performs in normal conditions if it already forms part of your garden. Is the tunnel sited on virgin land never previously used for cultivation, or is it situated on a bed you have used many times before? Whatever the case, it will do no harm to improve the fertility and the texture of the soil, by means of adding organic compost or well rotted farmyard manure just as you would normally. This addition will also help make the soil more moisture-retentive, which will play an important part under cover especially in the warmer months of the year.

If the soil has never been cultivated or has been previously laid to grass, keep a look out for pests like wireworms and leatherjackets. It is far better to sort out these problems now than later on when your vegetables have been sown and disturbing the soil is likely to cause problems.

If you are considering growing crops direct into the polytunnel soil, it is a good idea to check the pH level. If you have grown plants there before and they have been successful, then the pH is probably about right. Another good indicator is the presence of earthworms, which do not tolerate very acid soils. The ideal pH level for vegetables is about 6.5. This can be checked either with a soil testing kit available from garden centres or by getting a soil test carried out for you by a professional. He or she will be able to advise exactly what needs to be added to the soil to bring the pH to the correct level.

The growing area in your tunnel is finite so split the beds into imaginary or physically defined areas to maximise the space.

When preparing your soil, make sure that you eliminate all perennial weeds. As well as competing with your vegetables for nutrients and moisture, there is nothing more annoying, or potentially damaging to the plants you are trying to grow, than your having to disturb the soil to remove weed growth.

The growing area in your polytunnel is finite – and even in a large tunnel you will need to work out a rotation plan if you are growing a variety of crops. This will reduce the risk of disease and soil depletion caused by constant cultivation of the same or closely related plants grown in the same place year after year. Split your polytunnel beds into imaginary or physically defined areas and draw up a yearly rotation plan. Alternatively, you could replace the soil on a regular basis to avoid problems.

Which brings us on to the use of raised beds. The space available in your tunnel will dictate how big you can make your raised beds if you wish to use this method of growing. The possibilities are varied; do you want a large raised bed along one or both sides, or several smaller ones? Beds can be made cheaply from a variety of edgings: timber boards, railway sleepers, or weather-proof bricks, are just some of the possibilities. Using raised beds for your cultivation helps to define separate areas (making rotation plans simpler, as above), allows better drainage, and can be easily managed. The soil within each individual bed can be replaced or organic matter incorporated according to the needs of each crop.

One thing is certain in any polytunnel - undoubtedly, some weeds will find a way! If for example, seed trays and pots containing young plants are placed on the floor of the tunnel during the early part of the season, it is useful to place a sheet of woven weed suppressing material between the soil and the pots to eliminate weed growth.

Using grow bags and pots can eliminate the risk of pest and disease build-up, effectively 'resting' the soil. This is especially useful in the case of tomatoes, which grow very well in containers provided these are large enough, and adequate water and organic feed is given to the plants.

Repairing rips in the polythene.

One of the secrets of success for growing under cover is planning ahead. As well as deciding in advance which plants you would like to grow, draw up a yearly maintenance plan for the polytunnel itself. The best time of year for carrying out essential maintenance tasks is during the winter months when your tunnel will perhaps not be so full and when you are not as busy elsewhere in the garden.

Repairing rips in polythene, re-tensioning the sheet, and cleaning the cover inside and out are all jobs that need to be attended to on a regular basis.

Special wide transparent repair tape is available from polytunnel manufacturers and it is a good idea to always have a roll available for emergencies. The tape is just as effective for repairing small holes as it is larger rips and tears and is very strong, usually outlasting the polythene cover it is used to repair! For maximum adhesion ensure that the polythene is clean and dry before affixing the tape.

Whilst on the subject of repair, check that the door blinds or doors are in good working order. Due to the amount of use the doors get, they often require some kind of maintenance or even replacement from time to time. Better to get any potential problems sorted out early when you have plenty of time, rather than being forced to when that winter storm makes it a necessity!

## Top Tips

■ Remember one of the secrets of success for growing under cover is planning ahead.

■ Remember to always have a roll of repair tape ready.

Some tunnel hoops can be raised in the foundation tubes to re-tension the polythene cover if it has become slack. This is useful if your cover is still reasonably supple, but could cause problems if the polythene is several years old and more fragile.

Over time, the polythene cover will attract a film of algae and dirt. This can substantially reduce the light levels inside the tunnel, and should therefore be removed. To do this, first hose down the surface with water to soften the layer of dirt then use a soft brush or cloth to wipe it off. Hose down again and your tunnel will be much cleaner and more importantly, lighter! Don't forget to clean the inside surfaces too. You may also wish to use a organic disinfectant such as 'Citrox' to guard against disease.

Cleaning the cover inside and out are jobs that need to be attended to on a regular basis.

## Top Tips

■ Remember to clean the film of algae and dirt inside and outside regularly.

# Chapter 8

your polytunnel should be used for cultivation all year round.

## Under Cover through the Seasons

Polytunnels can and should be used for cultivation all year round. Admittedly, the bulk of activity will take place during spring and summer, but the protection of polythene can extend the growing season to last through the year if required. The relative comfort afforded to the gardener working inside is also likely to increase productivity!

Here is a season-by-season guide to growing in the polytunnel as well as a selection of the most popular and suitable crops for under cover cultivation. Alongside these are listed some of the more unusual plants to grow; now brought within the realms of possibility once one owns a polytunnel.

There is actually very little you can't grow in a polytunnel, but because space will always be limited, it is better to concentrate on those crops that do exceptionally well, or those that can only really thrive in a protected environment.

Regional climate differences still need to be taken into consideration, especially in the spring, just the same as plants grown outside. Normally, Southern gardeners will be able to start the season off 3 or 4 weeks earlier than their counterparts in the North.

Most crops prefer to be planted direct into the soil in the polytunnel. This gives the plants more room for root growth and offers the benefit of greater moisture retention. Organic grow-bags or large pots filled with organic compost suit certain plants very well but watering well and often is crucial as plants in confined spaces dry out much more quickly, especially in the heat of the summer. However, grow bags are definitely a good option to prevent soil sickness. This will happen if the tunnel stays in the same place and similar crops are grown in the same soil beds year after year. Alternatively, the soil inside the tunnel could be replaced periodically.

Early vegetables will be ready
for harvesting weeks earlier
than those outside.

Even during the cold winter months, the polytunnel can be productive. Autumn sown vegetables such as winter lettuce, spring kale and cabbage, Chinese greens, winter roots like turnip and carrot can all be harvested through the coldest months of the year. Look out for the varieties suitable for growing at this time. These can be cultivated without additional heating, but covering with fleece on very cold nights may be a requirement for some. Check the back of each seed packet for guidance. As space will not be so cramped, why not plant a few potato tubers, and look forward to enjoying delicious, freshly-dug new potatoes on Christmas Day!

## SPRING

Spring heralds a time of intense activity in the tunnel. As the temperature outside begins to rise, so the temperature inside the polytunnel can reach more than 25˚C/77˚F if the sun has been shining. The soil too will be warming up nicely. During the day ventilation will be needed. Night-time temperatures are still relatively cold, although this will not be a problem for those tunnels equipped with heating. Tender plants can always be protected by covering with fleece, bubble wrap or similar insulation material if frost is forecast.

This is the time to sow most of the vegetables to be harvested during the summer months, also flowers for cutting and for bedding. Cuttings can be taken from a wide variety of plants. A propagator is essential if these tasks are carried out in early spring, but if left until a few weeks later, the average temperature will have increased sufficiently for most seeds to germinate without the benefit of additional heating.

A real advantage of owning a polytunnel at this time of year is being able to sow early crops under protection in the soil beds. Early vegetables and fruit such as carrots, strawberries, radishes and salad crops to name a few will be ready for harvesting weeks earlier than those outside.

As the season progresses, young plants will need to be potted on before planting into their final positions.

## Top Tips

■ Remember that although protected you must still take regional climate conditions into account.

### Seed sowing

The polytunnel is an ideal place for growing plants from seed, especially if an electricity supply has been laid on which can be used to power electric propagators and heaters. This is more important during the very earliest months of the year when temperatures outside and in the tunnel will be low especially during the night. Most seed germination takes place between 12-20°C/55-68°F, and once the seedlings appear, an even temperature must be maintained to keep the plants growing on strongly.

In late March or early April, seeds can be sown in some of the unheated propagators or, if temperatures allow, simply in a seed tray covered with a sheet of glass. Depending on the weather, germination can be erratic but plants grown from seed later on can often catch up with those sown a week or so earlier, especially if the earlier ones receive a check due to low temperatures after they have been brought out of the propagator. Although harvested slightly later, there is no reason why vegetables raised without artificial heat will not provide as good a crop as ones sown earlier.

If growing from seed fit your tunnel with staging from the start.

If growing plants from seed and cuttings is going to be a major part of the activity in your own tunnel, why not divide part of it by installing an intermediate partition and door? One section could then be used as a designated propagation area fitted out with staging and all the associated items required for raising young plants. This area can then be heated more effectively without all the heat quickly dispersing all around the tunnel.

## Top Tips

■ Remember to maximise use of the tunnel to the full all year round.

## Taking cuttings

Raising new plants from cuttings is a cost effective and easy way to increase your stock. Softwood and hardwood cuttings can be successfully raised in the polytunnel. Softwood cuttings are taken during the spring or summer, generally speaking, the earlier the better to maximise the benefits of a longer growing season. To assist in the process of rooting, the stems of cuttings can be dipped in organic rooting powder before placed into the growing medium. In the case of extremely vigorous species such as members of the mint family, this is not necessary! The ideal growing medium for cuttings should be water retentive, incorporate air and be disease free. A mixture of perlite and peat or perlite and a good multi-purpose compost will fit the bill. Avoid damage to the stem of the cutting by making a small hole in the compost for it to go in. Keep the newly planted cuttings warm, and cover with a propagator lid or transparent polythene bag. On no account let the cuttings dry out.

- Softwood cuttings can be taken to increase stock of any shrubs, and these are taken from the young growing shoots or stems of the parent plant. As the name suggests, the cuttings are taken from soft, new plant growth. Softwood cuttings benefit from extra heat and once they have been potted, they can either be placed in a propagator or a polythene bag placed over the pot. In a couple of weeks or so the cuttings should show signs of new top growth and rooting.

- Semi hardwood cuttings are taken from the more mature shoots of plants but harvested from the parent plant so that part of the older woody stem is still attached. This part of the cutting is termed as a 'heel'. Semi hardwood cuttings are treated in the same way as softwood cuttings.

- Hardwood cuttings are made during the autumn and generally take longer to establish. They are ideally suited to raising in the polytunnel, and kept in there over the winter, ready to burst into life in the spring. The cuttings are taken from sections of stem from that year's growth. These sections should be between 20cm-24cm long and trimmed with secateurs or a sharp knife. The top of the stem should be cut just above a bud, and the bottom trimmed below a bud. Hardwood cuttings can be placed into pots for rooting as described earlier or inserted into a small trench lined with a little sharp sand at the bottom, then refilled. Unlike other types of cutting, they do not require additional heat, although care should be taken to keep them frost free over the winter.

## SUMMER

One thing is certain – there is always a lot going on in the polytunnel in summer! Much of the preparatory work done in the spring will be starting to pay off and you should begin to see the result in terms of fruit and vegetables cropping in abundance. The main requirements for growing during the summer will be water and good ventilation and this should be considered your main priority. Give the soil a good soaking twice a day – and keep a close watch on any seedlings still left in seed trays and pots which will dry out even faster.

Feeding should begin once the fruit has set on crops such as tomatoes and cucumbers, but leafy vegetables will also benefit from a regular dose of organic fertiliser. Constant vigilance will be needed to ensure pests and diseases do not take hold. If discovered early enough it will not take much to put things right. Remember when planting not to pack plants in together too tightly – and remove any damaged or dying leaves before disease and mould has a chance to set in. Above all, keep harvesting those vegetables to ensure they carry on cropping!

Lettuce and other salad vegetables can be sown all through the season; it is better to sow just a few seeds each week, ensuring that you won't experience a glut of everything at once, just an nice even spread of vegetables over the coming weeks. There is still time to plant a second crop of peas (choose an early variety) and French beans which will be ready for harvesting in late summer and early autumn. Look in the seed catalogues for the varieties of vegetables you can sow in late summer for cropping in autumn and over the winter.

## AUTUMN

In early autumn, there will still be much to be harvested, especially if you have made successful sowings over the last few months. Many vegetables suitable for overwintering in the polytunnel can be sown now, including kale, winter cabbage, winter lettuce, onions, etc.
The polytunnel can also be used for short term storing and drying of crops grown outside. I have found the space useful for drying onions before they are stored in net sacks for use over the winter. Tomatoes too can be left to ripen on their stems and hung from the roof bars for a while until needed.

Once plants have finished cropping, remove them before they start to decay.

The daily temperatures will be cooling now, and you can cut down on watering but ventilation is still very important to keep grey mould and other diseases which thrive in damp, still conditions at bay.

Autumn is an ideal time to take cuttings especially hedging plants, shrubs and tender perennials. Sweet peas can be sown in root trainers in the polytunnel during the autumn, and grown on through the winter. In February or March they will need to be planted into the soil bed ready for flowering in the spring.

## WINTER

Traditionally a time for gardeners and growers to take stock, review the last season and start planning for the next one. Things will be quietening down now in terms of growing, but some of the plants you raised from seed through late summer and early autumn will be ready now. Other plants will be overwintering in the tunnel ready for an early start next spring. Many of them will appreciate receiving an extra boost by way of an organic liquid feed.

Take a little time to get some polytunnel maintenance jobs out of the way. Dig over the soil and remove any old plant debris, weeds and anything else that could harbour or spread disease. Carry benching or staging outside and give it a thorough scrub before putting it back in the polytunnel. Resist the urge to use the tunnel to store old pots, bags of compost, seed trays, etc as they will soon become a hiding place for slugs and snails and other 'nasties'. Though not as convenient, it is much better to store these items in a secure garden shed.

Watering will only need to be done when absolutely necessary to reduce the damp conditions that mould and disease thrives in. Try to open the ventilation as much as possible if conditions allow – the circulation of air will help prevent fungal diseases.

Some hardy crops can be sown in pots in the tunnel in January and February such as broad beans and peas. In a few weeks they will be large enough to be planted outside. Early carrots can be sown in drills in the soil beds from February onwards.

Strawberries can be brought into the tunnel now for a crop produced at least 4 weeks earlier than those outside. Grow them in pots or put several in a grow-bag.

Tomatoes can be sown as early as January, but in as the temperature in most unheated tunnels will not be sufficiently high for them to survive outside the propagator, unless you can offer them a heated environment, it is better to play safe and wait until February.

## Top Tips

■ Remember the fitting of an intermediate door will allow you to heat only part of the tunnel.

The tomato is probably the most popular under cover crop – here planted with marigolds.

## FAVOURITE PLANTS FOR POLYTUNNELS:

Not surprisingly, many of the popular varieties grown in polytunnels are also firm favourites with greenhouse growers too.

### Tomatoes

Probably the most popular under cover crop, the tomato is a very worthwhile candidate for inclusion in the polytunnel. The delicious flavour of a home grown tomato bears no resemblance to the bland, watery offerings so often found in supermarkets. As well as the superior taste, growing your own tomatoes gives you the opportunity of trying different varieties, in varying shapes and colours. The salad bowl never looked or tasted more interesting!

Of course, tomatoes can be grown outside too, but they really come into their own in the polytunnel. Yields are higher and protection from the elements means they are more reliable. Pollination is not usually a problem in the enclosed space. The upright, cordon type of tomato (known as 'indeterminate'), rather than the bush ('determinate') varieties are an ideal choice if space is at a premium. Indeterminate varieties will need to have any side shoots removed on a regular basis which keeps the cordon shape and helps make the fruits reach maturity.

The ideal site for your tomato plants in the tunnel is direct into the soil bed. Watering thoroughly will ensure the moisture goes deep down. Some growers advocate letting tomatoes wilt slightly before watering again, but this is difficult if other plants are growing in close proximity. My own advice is to keep a happy medium. Alternatively, plant your tomatoes into growbags.

As they grow the tomato plants will need support. This can be provided by the traditional method of using bamboo canes or a similar upright support pushed into the soil near the base of the plant. Alternatively, strategic positioning of the plants directly underneath the frame of the polytunnel means that they can be supported by string tied to the frame. As the young fruits begin to set give the plants a dose of comfrey or seaweed liquid every two weeks or so. Once the lower trusses are well formed, remove some of the lower leaves to assist ripening.

Many gardening books recommend that tomato plants be 'stopped' by removing the growing tip once 5-7 trusses have been formed. This is said to encourage the remaining fruit to reach a greater size, although I have yet to be convinced. I let my plants reach the top of the tunnel if they can, forming several more trusses and have always been pleased with the results.

Tomato plants can easily be raised from seed and this is certainly the best way to experiment with different varieties. Alongside the most modern introductions, you could grow some of the older, 'heirloom' varieties still available. Most seed catalogues offer a good selection. The alternative is to buy young plants from a nursery or garden centre. The choice will not be as wide, but if you only require a plant or two, this may be a cost-effective way of obtaining them.

Heirloom varieties to try:
- Heirloom: Harbinger (1910)
- Golden Sunrise (1896)
- Red Brandywine (1800's)

Unusual varieties include:
- Yellow Pear
- Tigerella
- Black Russian

Reliable favourites:
- Gardener's Delight
- Alicante
- Shirley F1

Cucumbers, despite their reputation, thrive in the polytunnel.

## Cucumbers

This is another prolific crop for the polytunnel and just one plant can produce enough cucumbers for a family over the summer months. Cucumbers have a reputation of being difficult to grow, but once established and given plenty of water, they do not need too much extra care. The easiest varieties of all are the all-female ones – the seed is more expensive to buy, but well worth it. The older types such as 'Telegraph' need the male flowers removing as they cause the fruits to become bitter if left on the plant. Having said that, the effort is still worth it as the older varieties tend to be slightly more hardy and are still very popular with many gardeners.

As with tomatoes, the choice will be wider if you grow your own plants from seed, but young plants can be bought. Choose the healthiest, sturdiest young plants you can – cucumbers have a tendency to 'stretch' if not given enough light or grown too closely together in the early stages. All varieties will need supporting – this needs to be fairly robust as plants usually produce several cucumbers at a time and will be considerably heavy.

Cucumber seed does require higher temperatures to germinate (minimum 20°C/68°F), and once the seedlings are out of the propagator, good light and a temperature of no less than 15°C/60°F to ensure strong, productive plants.

### A selection of varieties includes:

| | | | |
|---|---|---|---|
| **All Female:** | Carmen F1, | Petita F1, | Cumlaude F1, |
| **Male/female:** | Telegraph, | Conqueror, | Tanja |

## Aubergines

The egg plant has become a more popular crop in recent years, probably due to the interest in more exotic dishes than was the norm a decade or two ago. The plants can take up quite some room and should be spaced well apart (60cm/2ft) if planted into the soil. Aubergines are related to tomatoes, peppers and potatoes so can fall prey to the same pests and diseases. This fact also needs to be taken into consideration when rotating crops around the tunnel each year.

The seed will germinate at a temperature of 20 °C/68°F and the young plants will need potting on until early summer when they can be planted into the soil bed or into grow bags or 8 inch pots. Aubergines do need support and this can be given by growing them up canes and tying in side shoots as they develop. The fruits are quite large compared to the size of the plant and so each plant should be restricted to five or six fruits each, this can be done by removing excess flowers.

Aubergines like plenty of light, a humid atmosphere and lots of water. Their feeding requirements are similar to that of tomatoes. The fruits are ready for harvesting when the surface becomes shiny.

### Varieties to look for:

- Black Beauty
- Long Purple
- Moneymaker F1

Both chilli (shown here) and sweet peppers are suitable for growing in the polytunnel.

## Peppers

These are divided into two types: chilli and sweet peppers and both are suitable for growing in the polytunnel. Both types require the same methods of cultivation. Before planting peppers, work in plenty of well rotted compost into the soil bed or use organic growbags.

They are relatively easy to grow and once they are planted into their final positions, they do not need supporting, removal of side shoots or of the growing tip ('stopping'). They need to be kept moist but not over-watered. Feed each week using an organic feed such as liquid seaweed. Peppers are not generally prone to pests and diseases.

Pepper seeds need to be sown in late March or early April in a propagator at 21°C/70°F.

■ Sweet Pepper:
These are the larger, fatter and milder tasting variety. Green, red and yellow peppers come from the same plant! The fruits turn from green to red and yellow as they mature.

■ Chilli Pepper:
The narrower, hot-tasting variety. Use sparingly, especially the red ones!

## Commercial Crops in Tunnels

The popularity of the polytunnel for growing commercial crops has expanded rapidly in the last decade. It is estimated that over the last five to six years over 2000 acres of commercial polytunnels have been constructed in the UK. The many advantages polytunnel cultivation gives to growers are higher yields, earlier season crops, secure all year round production, drier crop conditions and less wet-weather diseases such as botrytis and the bonus of guaranteed harvest days. Work can go on in the tunnel unaffected by the weather conditions outside and the large size of many tunnels means that heavy machinery can be brought in to carry out certain tasks. The growing environment can be tailor made to suit any crop by adjustments to the heating, ventilation and irrigation systems – which in many of the larger operations are controlled completely by computer.

The variety of crops grown commercially in polytunnels is almost as wide as the choice grown outside. The versatility of the modern tunnel renders it ready for practically any growing purpose: plants can be grown in a completely enclosed environment, or if the weather or the crop requires it, ventilation can be such that it matches the conditions outside at certain times. Some of the most recent advances in polytunnel design have produced structures which are equipped with roll-up roofs, providing completely natural ventilation when needed.

Many plants not normally associated with the British climate can be grown successfully. Here melon 'Green Nutmeg' thrives.

## Unusual plants for Polytunnels

Many plants which cannot be grown outside in the British climate can be successfully raised under cover and will produce fruit. Why not give some of them a try? Just a few examples are Cape Gooseberry, Okra, melons and the more tender varieties of grape.

Of course there are also many perennial house plants and other exotics suitable for growing in the tunnel in the summer, but these will need heated conditions in the winter.

## FLOWERS:

The polytunnel offers ideal growing conditions for flowers, especially those grown for cutting. The plants are protected from the elements and blooms of exhibition quality can be achieved. Many different types of flower can be grown, for example, sweet pea, chrysanthemum, carnation, sweet william. Choose from the varieties recommended especially for cutting and display purposes in the seed catalogues or young plants offered at specialist nurseries.

As the taller plants grow, you will need to devise some sort of support by using netting or by making your own. Crop bars attached to the polytunnel frame provide a sturdy point for fixing your supports.

## OTHER PLANTS

Courgettes and marrows mature weeks earlier than outside but they do take up a lot of space.

Courgettes and marrows do very well in a polytunnel, maturing weeks earlier than outside. Unfortunately, they do take up a lot of space, so if you are growing them outside too, it is perhaps better to sacrifice the one or two grown under cover (this will be more than enough) once the outdoors ones start cropping. Courgettes and marrows need copious amounts of water to allow fruit development.

One of the most rewarding herbs to grow in the tunnel, basil, really thrives in the warm, protected environment due to its Mediterranean origins. There are many interesting varieties: purple, sweet, cinnamon, lemon, bush. Basil is also the perfect accompaniment to tomatoes so why not grow them together?

Another herb which grows well under cover is parsley. New plants can be sown during the summer, planted up in the polytunnel, and will provide a crop all through the winter.

Lettuces take up little space and the list of varieties is huge. As well as differently coloured leaves and varying shapes: cos, loose leaf, salad bowl, iceberg, there are other crops suitable for the use in salads such as corn salad, endive, chicory, and mizuna. These are all easily grown.

Radishes can be rewarding in a polytunnel but only if sown early – the temperature in the summer will quickly become too hot for them to flourish. As radishes are fast maturing, it is possible to get a decent crop early in the season.

One of the most valuable benefits of owning a polytunnel is being able to harvest early-sown vegetables during the early summer when home grown produce is in short supply. Early crops, such as carrots and spinach can be sown direct into the tunnel soil in February ready for cropping in June. Look out especially for early, fast-maturing varieties. There are many other types of vegetable suitable for growing at this time and choice really does depend on personal preference.

The beehive – the ultimate in pollination strategy?

## PLANTS STARTED OFF IN THE TUNNEL

The polytunnel is an ideal place to start off any plants destined for life in the great outdoors. From bedding to brassicas, peas to French beans, any vegetable suitable for transplanting at a later date can be sown inside from seed. Even some root vegetables which have a reputation for poor transplanting can be grown in root trainers ensuring their roots will not be disturbed when replanted outside.

## COMPANION PLANTING

This is the term used for growing different plants in close proximity for certain benefits. It is completely natural and is therefore an ideal method to use alongside other organic measures. For example, French marigolds (Tagetes) planted next to tomatoes, will attract hoverflies which in turn prey on aphids, a major pest of tomatoes. The scent of marigolds can also be put to good use in deterring certain pests by disguise. Scientific trials discovered that the cabbage white butterfly seeks out brassicas by scent and aromatic French marigolds close by will confuse them. Similarly, onions planted alongside carrots will help deter carrot root fly for the same reason.

A useful combination for the polytunnel is the planting of dill near young cucumber plants. Dill's delicate ferny leaves will protect the cucumber from potential sun-scorch. Once the cucumber is big enough to fend for itself, the dill can be picked and used in salads, too. Garlic is said to protect strawberry crops from grey mould.

## POLLINATION

If you keep your polytunnel well ventilated through the summer months, you can expect that the pollination of your crops will be successful. Leave the doors at each end open to allow beneficial insects free access. If you are using French marigolds in your companion planting scheme, these will also attract hoverflies and other useful insects into the tunnel to assist with pollination. The beehive next to my polytunnel may probably look to be the ultimate in pollination strategy – in fact the bees rarely venture inside the tunnel! Sadly, the varieties typically grown there are not at the top of a honeybee's list of favourite food plants and the polytunnel simply creates a sheltered spot for the hive!

## WATERING

Water is one of the most fundamental requirements in the polytunnel. There are many ways of supplying water to your plants and this really depends on your own preference and on the size of your polytunnel. In smaller tunnels watering cans, hand held hoses or seep or trickle hoses are quite adequate; for the larger sizes, an overhead irrigation system is more practical.

The water supply can be rainwater or straight from the mains water supply. Many larger tunnels are equipped with huge water storage tanks and in a smaller tunnel the same principle can be used by keeping a water butt or similar container in the tunnel filled with water from an outside source. However, this needs to be completely emptied and refilled on a regular basis, as the water inside can soon become contaminated with bacteria and algae especially in the summer.

Work out a watering regime. This will vary through the seasons and will be affected by the air temperature and sunshine levels. The types of plants inside and their individual requirements will also play a major part in determining the quantities of water required. Once this has been established, that might be the time to have a re-think on your ideal method of irrigation!

It is can be just as serious not to over-water as it is to under-water, especially in colder weather as wet soil won't dry out as quickly and can soon lead to fungal diseases like botrytis and similar damp related problems. A moisture meter can be used to check moisture levels, but an experienced 'tunneller' will get soon get a feel for what feels right.

During a hot summer, copious amounts of water will be needed. A good soaking is more beneficial than a light sprinkling over the surface of the soil beds as simply wetting the top of the soil causes it to form a hard crust, making water penetration in future much more difficult.

## MAKING YOUR OWN ORGANIC FEED

If you have prepared the soil in your polytunnel by incorporating lots of organic material – with either compost from your compost heap or well-rotted farmyard manure, soil fertility will be high. This is one of the fundamentals of organic gardening. However, certain crops will benefit from extra feeding to encourage flowers and fruit to form. Tomatoes are an example.

Ready made organic liquid fertilisers can be bought for the purpose, but you can make your own. Nettles, comfrey and manure can all be used to make liquid fertiliser. I use all three in my own garden. All you need is a large bin or water butt (one with a tap at the bottom for draining off the liquid when needed is ideal), raised off the ground with bricks. Half fill the butt with water, then, add a large quantity of either nettle or comfrey leaves. Leave for a week or so, until the leaves start to break down in the liquid. Give it a quick stir and the liquid is then ready for use. A word of warning - the resulting liquid smells rather pungent!

Liquid manure is made in a similar way – simply fill half a hessian sack (or for a smaller quantity, a pair of ladies tights) with manure (horse, sheep, cow, pig or goat can be used) and secure the top tightly with string. The string can then be tied around a length of wood slightly longer than the top of the water butt so that the sack is suspended in the water. The liquid manure is ready in a week or two.

You can make your own wormery using a plastic rubbish bin.

## WORM COMPOSTING

Another string to the polytunnel fertility bow is the production of worm compost. The compost that worms produce is full of nutrients, and although even a large worm bin will only produce a limited quantity of material, if it is incorporated into seed beds, around newly planted crops or as an ingredient in seed or potting composts, it is a valuable asset in the polytunnel.

Wormeries can be purchased as a complete kit with bin and worms or can be made easily enough from a plastic rubbish bin. This needs to have drainage holes drilled at the bottom and ventilation at the top along with a lid to keep it waterproof. The worms themselves are 'brandling' or 'tiger worms' sold in fishing tackle shops as bait. Their main requirement in the worm bin is some bedding material and food. The bedding material is placed at the bottom of the bin and is made up of old garden compost, manure, and damp shredded newspaper. The worms can then be added and a very small layer of 'food' placed on top. Food for the worms consists of kitchen scraps (not meat), garden waste and damp shredded newspapers. This should never be more than a couple of centimetres deep at a time. Keep the contents moist, not waterlogged. Don't forget to check the food supply regularly, topping up with more once the original quantity is almost gone. Depending on the time of year, this can take 2-4 weeks.

Site the wormery in a sheltered spot, away from full sun in summer and protected from frost in winter. If it is suitable, why not put it near your polytunnel? Look at the contents of the bin every few weeks to check progress of the compost. When there is a reasonable amount it can be used, but don't forget to separate to worms and return them to the wormery to start the process again!

Hanging baskets can be started from scratch by growing all the plants required from seed.

The central ridge pole creates a natural spot to support your hanging baskets until danger of frost is over.

# HANGING BASKETS AND CONTAINERS

Hanging baskets and other containers for summer displays can be started from scratch in the polytunnel by growing all the plants required from seed, raising them from cuttings, or by purchasing young plants from a nursery and growing them on. If it is early in the season always protect the young plants from risk of frost by covering them with fleece overnight.

It is then up to you to choose the moment to plant up your basket or other container. Larger baskets are easier to manage once outside as they retain moisture for longer than the smaller ones. Use an environmentally friendly basket liner made from materials such as coir fibre, recycled cardboard or moss grown specifically for gardening use (not taken from the wild) and a good organic compost.

The advantage of a polytunnel is that the newly planted basket can be suspended from the central ridge bar until it can go outside, either to mature and fill the basket so it goes into its final position in optimum condition, or because the weather outside is not quite warm enough. Whatever the reason, don't forget about them and give them plenty of water and feed just as you would when they are outside!

To keep your containers and baskets looking good right through the season, water frequently, once a day may not be enough, especially on hot summer days when the plants can dry out really quickly. A quick check to feel how heavy a basket is will tell you if it requires water or not. Feeding needs to be done at least twice a week especially when the plants have been in their containers or baskets for some time. Finally, don't forget to keep dead-heading the old flowers to ensure your plants continue blooming for weeks to come.

# Chapter 9

# Pest Control

To a certain extent a polytunnel will protect your crops from those pests usually encountered outside. Pigeons and rabbits will not venture in to wreak their usual havoc! Other nuisances such as carrot root fly, a serious pest on carrots grown outside, are rarely seen inside tunnels. This is due to their being unable to locate the crop. On the other hand a polytunnel can also provide an ideal environment for certain other troubles due to the high humidity and temperature created within.

As an organic gardener I find preventative measures are more preferable than having to tackle pest or disease problems when they strike. Strong, healthy plants are more likely to be able to fend off an attack. Cleanliness in the polytunnel will also help. Remove any damaged leaves before they decay and become a target for disease. Keep the soil weed-free — not only will your plants be healthier, not having to compete for nutrients, but weed growth can also harbour pests and diseases.

The polytunnel will protect your crops from some of the pests usually encountered outside.

Try to resist the urge to store old pots, sacks of compost, empty seed trays, tools and the like in the tunnel as they can become a refuge for all manner of pests. Slugs and snails in particular like to hide away during the day and will come out at night to feast on your vegetables! Benching or staging can also provide a safe haven for pests so have a thorough check underneath from time to time.

Plastic traps filled with beer make very effective slug traps.

Pests and diseases can also reside in the soil itself. By practising crop rotation in your tunnel you will limit the build up of disease which would be likely to occur if the same crop were grown in the same place year after year.

Equally, the plants will not be affected by nutrient deficiency, making them stronger, healthier and therefore more disease resistant.

Let's have a look at a few of the most common pests and diseases that you may be unlucky enough to encounter 'under cover'. For more in-depth disease diagnoses and organic remedies, consult the publications listed in the appendix at the end of this book.

Slugs and snails:

These are a very common problem in the polytunnel environment. The damage one slug can cause to a row of young seedlings in one night is enormous. Slugs and snails thrive in the sheltered, often damp conditions and preventative measures are the best way to stop these creatures taking hold. Natural predators such as birds and hedgehogs are unlikely to enter the polytunnel to help control the mollusc population but if you have a pond nearby, the occasional visit from a toad or frog may help. Try to avoid watering during the evening and go on periodic 'slug hunts' – especially at night by torchlight! The slugs and snails can then be picked up and disposed of.

## Top Tips

■ Remember to check all plants before they are introduced into the polytunnel for signs of disease or pests.

Mixing up 'Nemaslug' control ready for use.

There are many organic traps and deterrents available including biological controls. Plastic traps filled with beer such as the one shown here are very effective; these can be bought from most garden centres or you can make your own from plastic cartons or glass jars sunk into the ground.

Crushed egg shells or coarse grit can be sprinkled around individual plants as slugs and snails dislike crawling over dry surfaces, but these will not work if the material is wet. Other 'barrier' controls come in the form of collars ready-made from plastic or copper, which surround the plant to protect it from attack. You can make your own collars using old plastic bottles.

Biological control comes in the form of nematodes, microscopic organisms that seek out and kill slugs, reproducing inside them. This control can only be used in the warmer months of the year when the temperature in the tunnel is between 10°C (55°F) and 25°C (77°F). It is most effective for killing young slugs under the soil surface and each application lasts up to six weeks. See the suppliers list in the appendix on details of how to obtain this product, known as 'Nemaslug.' This will not control snails.

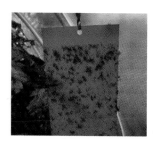

Sticky yellow traps do attract whitefly
but often at the expense
of other, beneficial, insects.

## Whitefly/Aphids:

Another host of common pests found in polytunnels and greenhouses are whitefly and aphids (greenfly and blackfly). These cause damage by sucking sap and weakening the plants that they infest. Living on the underside of leaves, whitefly is easily seen flying about when the plants are disturbed. Greenfly and blackfly cluster on the stems and especially on young shoots which eventually become distorted and die back.

The aphid is a major source of food for other insects such as ladybirds (both in its adult and larval stage), lacewing and hoverfly larvae and beetles. However, sometimes the aphid population will be so great that natural predation is not sufficient to keep the pests at bay. If the aphids are detected at an early stage, and you are not too squeamish they could be squashed and destroyed by hand.

Sticky yellow traps are often employed to attract whiteflies and these do work, but often at the expense of other beneficial insects which are also attracted and come to a sticky end. Yellow traps should certainly never be used after the introduction of flying biological controls.

Try companion planting using French marigolds 'Tagetes' in the tunnel, especially around tomatoes – the strong scent acts as a repellent. A mixture of soft soap and water can be applied using a hand sprayer. This is effective against aphids and whitefly, if used before the infestation becomes too severe.

As soon as the first pests are discovered, biological controls can be used. This form of pest control simply works by introducing one species in order to control another. There is no risk to beneficial insects or humans or pets. Encarsia (a small parasitic wasp) or Delphastus (a relative of the ladybird) are used to control whitefly and Aphidius (a tiny insect which lays its eggs directly into its prey) for greenfly and blackfly. Alternatively, ladybird larvae can be purchased. Ladybird adults and larvae are voracious consumers of aphids and a single ladybird can eat up to 5000 aphids during its lifetime. The controls need to be introduced during the warmer months to be effective.

There are certain safer pesticides that can be used under an organic system. These are currently approved by the organic standards authorities for use in the UK. Pyrethrum and Derris are both effective against aphids and can be used in powder or liquid form. Care needs to be taken when applying as they can harm both beneficial insects and fish.

### Red Spider Mite:

If the leaves on your cucumber plants start to look dried out and yellow, take a closer look. Are the leaves covered in fine cobwebs? These are symptoms of a serious polytunnel pest, red spider mite. The mites themselves are minute and difficult to see and unfortunately the hot, dry conditions in a polytunnel suit them perfectly. Left to their own devices, red spider will severely weaken plants and reduce the crop. In extreme cases, the plants will die. These pests can attack a wide variety of plants, but cucumbers and climbing French beans are their favourites.

To fend off an attack before it takes hold, try making the atmosphere in the tunnel cooler and more humid by spraying the plants regularly with water. Using a soft soap fatty acid spray should help if used early enough.

Once the temperatures have risen above 10°C/55°F, biological controls can be used. Phytoseiulus persimilis is a predator mite which feeds on the red spider mite. Once established, these predators will ensure good control of the mites throughout the growing season.

## Botrytis/Grey Mould:

Generally, not so much of a problem during the summer, grey mould thrives in the cooler damper conditions present in the polytunnel during the autumn and winter. Look out for the tell-tale signs - greyish mould on leaves and stems and die back. To stop the spread of the disease, remove all damaged and diseased plant material, and burn it. Try to ventilate the polytunnel as much as possible.

This is just one of several fungal diseases which can occur; downy mildew, powdery mildew and blight are others you may encounter. Fungal diseases are airborne and blight spores in particular can travel some distance. Tomatoes are very susceptible to blight and tomatoes and potatoes (which are close relations of the tomato) affected outside can transfer the disease into the tunnel if not sited far enough away (or out of wind direction).

## Mosaic Virus:

Although there are many different types of plant viruses, Mosaic Virus is one of the most common on plants grown under cover. The disease is normally spread by aphids and can be detected in its early stages by the yellowing of the younger leaves first, then the older ones. Once the virus has taken hold, there is not much you can do. Try to control aphid numbers in the tunnel at all times.

This is not meant to be an exhaustive list of the ailments your plants may suffer, just some of the most common to affect polytunnel cultivation. Consult a specialist gardening publication if the symptoms are not listed here. If you are lucky you may not see too many of them and certainly not all at once! As with all pests and disease problems, prevention is better than cure. Practice good tunnel hygiene and get into the habit of checking your plants every day. Be vigilant when introducing new plants into the tunnel to ensure they are healthy and not carriers of anything untoward. Try using some of the new disease resistant varieties. Give your plants plenty of room – this will help with ventilation, and they will be all the stronger for not having to compete with each other for light, moisture and nutrients. Healthy plants equal happy growers!

## Top Tips

■ Remember to check all plants before they are introduced into the polytunnel for signs of disease or pests.

NOTES

NOTES

**Chapter 10**

# Polytunnels work for them!

What makes different people choose polytunnels? The versatility of these structures enables them to be used for many different reasons and for a variety of uses. This book has concentrated mainly on the polytunnel as a medium for crop growing, but is also used for other things. Here we take a look at four individuals, all successfully using polytunnels.

Gary Beaman, a smallholder from Lincolnshire, has used his 18ft x 30' polytunnel for two years to over winter his flock of Ryeland sheep and for the purpose of lambing in the spring. Gary's tunnel was purchased especially as a sheep shelter and is clad in opaque polythene to diffuse the light and keep the temperature cooler inside. Around all the sides from ground level to 1 metre high, high tensile cladding is used as reinforcement – a necessity when using a polytunnel for any kind of livestock. Ventilation is achieved using double doors at each end providing a through draught. These look rather like stable doors, as the top can be opened while the bottom half remains shut. A native hedge is planted 8 feet away and provides an effective windbreak. The inside of the polytunnel is fitted out with sheep hurdles and CCTV so that any activity can be observed from inside the house. This is of course very important during the lambing season.

Have there been any problems with the polytunnel? Only when it first arrived – unfortunately the booklet explaining how to erect the tunnel had a page missing and the kit arrived with all the fixings for a 70' long tunnel which proved very confusing.

'Aveland Trees' have used polytunnels since the company was founded in the 1980s.

Gary's tunnel works well for him now however, and he is currently considering raising turkeys in it during the summer and autumn when the sheep are outside.

Hugh Dorrington founded Aveland Trees 15 years ago. The company which is based in Lincolnshire specialises in growing British native trees and hedging all of which are raised from seed. Much of the demand for hedging comes from the local area and across East Anglia.

From the outset, polytunnels were used, in fact three out of six of the original 18' x 54' structures are still in use today. Being native species, the majority of cultivation is carried on outside, however, the tunnels are put to use when the autumn sown seeds are moved in over the winter. No heating is necessary and the doors at either end of the tunnels are left open all the time. This inhibits early growth which could cause problems once the seedling trees are moved back outside in the spring. The polythene is a standard grade and covers generally last about 5 years.

From June onwards, holly is moved into the tunnel. Again, the doors are left open to provide as much ventilation as possible and the manually operated overhead irrigation keeps the plants watered. One of the tunnels is currently covered in green mesh and houses yew saplings which seem to prefer rather more shade than the other species.

So has Hugh experienced any problems with his polytunnels over the years? All are situated in a sheltered yard and so are not too affected by adverse weather conditions. The biggest problem he has had was with the trenches dug for burying the polythene. Due to the fairly light soil, any heavy rain washed both the soil and the polythene out of the trenches! To overcome this, a metal strip was attached all around the inside of the frame about 3 inches above soil level. The polythene was then stretched over the structure in the usual way and plastic retaining strips pushed into grooves in the metal strip from outside holding the polythene firmly in place. The excess polythene is still buried in the ground but now stays where it is supposed to.

Piers Warren, an organic smallholder who lives in Norfolk has been using his 10' x 12' polytunnel for 5 years. Covered in Visqueen thermal non-drip polythene, the tunnel is of standard construction with the hoops spaced 6 feet apart. It is ventilated at both ends, one end with an opening door, the other end with a ventilation flap. The instructions received with the polytunnel were not very easy to follow and erecting it was therefore not straightforward, but once it was up it soon became a very important part of the smallholding.

As an advocate of self-sufficiency, Piers' tunnel is used right through the year for growing a selection of vegetables to supplement the ones he grows outdoors. Favourites that feature in the polytunnel are tomatoes, cucumbers, Chinese cabbage, French beans in the summer months, and early season crops of lettuce, radish, spring onion, courgette and potatoes grown in pots. In the winter, kale is grown in the tunnel, making it truly a year round asset. The only crops which have proved slightly disappointing have been aubergines, capsicums and okra.

Watering is carried out manually with a watering can filled from a water butt.

Similar to the views of other polytunnel owners, Piers rates his polytunnel highly and if he had to buy another one, not surprisingly he would choose the same design but BIGGER. That's the only problem with a polytunnel, whatever size you have it's never quite large enough!

David Nieburg and Jo Taylor began growing potted herbs in an 18' x 64' polytunnel they inherited when they moved into their previous home in 1998. Fairly soon after they bought another, larger tunnel measuring 27' x 64'. Since then their company, Country Herbs and Plants, has gone from strength to strength and now supplies more than 100 varieties of herb to wholesalers and garden centres up and down the country.

The move to new premises in 2001 heralded another change to a multi-span tunnel, with an overall covered area of 1300 square metres. The new polytunnel was positioned alongside a similar size glasshouse, used for growing African violets and owned by David's father. The size of the polytunnel was chosen to mirror the dimensions of the glasshouse, so that any accessories such as irrigation pipes could be used in either structure if needed. The polytunnel is covered in Luminance UVI thermal polythene sheeting on the roof which gives a screening effect, keeping the tunnel cooler than the standard grade covers. This makes it less likely to scorch the plants inside.

A view inside 'Country Herbs and Plants' multispan tunnel.

On this scale, professionals will come and erect the tunnel for you. With such a large polytunnel, the ventilation and irrigation methods had to be carefully planned. An overhead irrigation system, supplied from a large reservoir which collects rainwater from the roof gutters was installed. This is used in conjunction with a hose pipe system, the pipe is connected to the roof frame on each span which allows for spot watering of any plants needing special attention.

Ventilation is an even more integral part of the polytunnel and this is made possible with a gap in the polythene that runs all the way around the structure one metre from ground level. Covering this gap is what is basically a polythene blind that can be rolled up or down by means of a winding gear thus opening and closing the vents. Each side is manually controlled separately from the others, allowing for different sides to be open or closed depending on the wind direction.

Originally the floor of the polytunnel was covered with sand, but problems with weed growth meant that 'Mypex' woven sheeting was used instead.

As already mentioned, the tunnel had to be sited parallel to the existing glasshouse. For a year after it was erected, the polytunnel had no hedge or any sort of windbreak to protect it from the winds that whipped across the surrounding fields. The following winter a heavy gale tore a hole in one corner of the tunnel with dire consequences – part of the polythene roof on one span was ripped off. Of course, it could have been a whole lot worse...

To stop this happening again, a windbreak was erected using telegraph poles and heavy-duty plastic windbreak netting around the three exposed sides. Other growers in the area employ the same method, so this should be effective.

Are there any hints and tips for using a polytunnel on this scale? David stresses that when preparing the site, correct ground levels are even more important as there is more scope for error – a slight deviation at one end can develop into a major discrepancy at the other! If he were buying another tunnel would he choose the same again? Probably, although he feels that a smaller span could be more easily ventilated. The centre of his existing polytunnel is very difficult to ventilate due to the large area, even using overhead circulatory fans.

NOTES

NOTES

# The Polytunnels companion checklists

Set out below are just some of the questions you should be considering when planning your polytunnel.

1. What will the tunnel be used for?  Plant cultivation or keeping livestock?

2. If for growing — is it for protected cultivation under polythene or as a fruit cage/net protection for other crops?

3. On what scale will it be utilised?  For domestic use only or for small or large scale commercial enterprises?  This will dictate size and type of structure.

4. Your budget:  Go for the largest size you can afford, as generally polytunnels become relatively cheaper metre for metre the bigger they are.

5. Polythene:  Will the tunnel be heated during the winter? Thermal grade polythene is more heat-retentive.
   If growing frost hardy plants, standard grade should be adequate.

6.  Larger tunnels need additional ventilation.  Consider ridge vents or mesh vent panel along sides.

7.  What will be grown?  Crop bars may be useful for supporting some plants.  Straight-sided tunnels give wider working area — necessary if using benches/staging along sides.

8.  Irrigation:  Will watering with a can or a hose pipe be adequate, or is an irrigation system a definite requirement?

9.  Exposed or sheltered site?  May need strengthened frame, closer hoop spacing if in wind prone area.

10. Soil type: Heavy or light?  Will dictate method of securing foundation tubes into soil.  If light and sandy, cementing tubes in place may be necessary.

Questions to ask your supplier.

As well as supplying your polytunnel, your chosen supplier should be able to confidently answer any questions or concerns you might have as well as suggesting the polytunnel that best suits your needs and situation if you need guidance. Here is a selection of questions you may wish to ask:

## A. Polytunnel Suitability to your needs

1. Is the polytunnel you have chosen right for your particular needs?

2. Is it suitable for your particular site? If you live in an exposed location, can they offer suggestions to make the structure more secure?

3. Can additional features i.e. ventilation, internal doors, etc., be added at a later date?

## B. Polytunnel Construction

1. Does the polytunnel kit come with detailed instructions for construction?

2. Do they offer a telephone helpline for advice if you get stuck during the construction process? Is this out of hours, what cost is the call per minute.

3. If you don't intend erecting the polytunnel yourself can they recommend a local contractor to do this for you?

C. Cost of the polytunnel.

1. Does this include all the basic items; for example –
   Anti Hot Spot tape or timber and materials needed to
   construct the doors?

2. What about the cost of any optional extras such as
   ventilation panels and irrigation pipes?

3. Is delivery included in the price?

4. What guarantees for polythene and frame do they give?

## INDEX

| | |
|---|---|
| Anti Hot Spot tape | 22,42 |
| Aphids | 74 |
| Aubergine | 61 |
| Basil | 65 |
| Biological control | 73,75 |
| Botrytis | 76 |
| Cape Gooseberry | 64 |
| Cleaning | 50 |
| Climate | 21,27 |
| Commercial polytunnels | 9,28,30,32,63,30,82 |
| Companion planting | 66,74 |
| Containers | 70 |
| Courgettes | 65 |
| Crop bars | 21,36 |
| Cucumbers | 60 |
| Cuttings | 54-55 |
| Doors | 24,49 |
| Erecting the polytunnel | 39,44 |
| Feeding | 68 |
| Flowers | 64 |
| Greenhouses | 11,12,16 |
| Grow bags | 48,51,58 |
| Hanging baskets | 15,70 |
| Heavy duty tunnels | 21 |
| Heaters | 34-35 |
| Irrigation | 31-32 |
| Lettuce | 65 |
| Livestock in tunnels | 18,79 |
| Maintenance | 49 |
| Marigold | 66 |
| Marrows | 65 |
| Melons | 64 |
| Mesh | 24 |

| | |
|---|---|
| Mosaic virus | 76 |
| Multi span tunnels | 20 |
| Okra | 64 |
| Parsley | 65 |
| Paths | 44 |
| Peppers, Chilli | 62 |
| Peppers, Sweet | 62 |
| pH level | 47 |
| Pigeons | 71 |
| Planning permission | 27 |
| Plant Supports | 36 |
| Pollination | 66 |
| Polythene grades | 22-24 |
| Polytunnel beds | 47-48 |
| Polytunnel, types of | 17,20 |
| Rabbits | 71 |
| Radish | 65 |
| Raised beds | 48 |
| Red spider mite | 75 |
| Repairs | 49 |
| Secondhand polytunnels | 25 |
| Seeds | 53 |
| Slugs | 72-73 |
| Snails | 72-73 |
| Soil | 47 |
| Staging | 35 |
| Temperature in the tunnel | 25,28 |
| Thermometers | 36 |
| Tomatoes | 58-59 |
| Ventilation | 24-25 |
| Watering | 67 |
| Weed suppressing materials | 48 |
| Whitefly | 74 |
| Wind conditions | 12,21,27 |
| Windbreaks | 21,29 |
| Worm compost | 69 |

## Photo Credits

Acknowledgements and grateful thanks go to First Tunnels, and Ferryman Polytunnels and National Poly tunnels for their help in providing the following photographs:

First Tunnels: Pages 20,24,25,27,31,32,34,35,42, back cover
Ferryman Polytunnels: Pages 12,18,28, back cover
Stair Organics: Page 14
Author photograph: John Neville
All other photographs: Jayne Neville

## Further reading

**Gardening Under Plastic,** Bernard Salt (Batsford )
**Grow your own Vegetables,** Joy Larcombe (Frances Lincoln Ltd)
**The Organic Bible,** Bob Flowerdew (Kyle Cathie)
**Organic Gardening,** Geoff Hamilton (Dorling Kindersley)
**Pests – How to Control them on Fruit and Vegetables** (organic), Pears & Sherman (HDRA)
**River Cottage Cookbook,** Hugh Fearnley-Whittingstall (Harper Collins)

## Polytunnel Manufacturers and Accessories

First Tunnels Limited, Dixon Street, Barrowford, Lancashire BB9 8PL. Tel. 01282 601253
www.firsttunnels.co.uk

Ferryman Polytunnels, Bridge Road, Lapford, Crediton, Devon EX17 6AE . Tel. 01363 83444
www.ferryman.com

Wychwood Polytunnels, Rudford, Gloucester GL2 8DY. Tel. 01452 790650

Clovis Lande, Branbridge Road,
East Peckham, Tonbridge, Kent TN12 5HH.
Tel.01622 873900 www.clovis.co.uk

Multi-Mesh, PO Box 24, Callington,
Cornwall PL17 7YF Tel. 01822 833036

## Polythene Manufacturers
Visqueen, PO Box 343, Yarm Road, Stockton on Tees,
Cleveland TS18 3GE Tel. 01642 672288.

## Suppliers: Seeds and Sundries
Organic Gardening Catalogue, Riverdene Business Park,
Molesey Road, Hersham, Surrey KT12 4RG.
Tel 01932 253666 www.OrganicCatalog.com
(organic seeds, pest control, sundries)

Suffolk Herbs, Monks Farm, Coggeshall Road,
Kelvedon, Essex. Tel. 01376 572456 www.suffolkherbs.com
(organic seed supplier, gardening sundries)

S.E. Marshall & Co. Ltd, Wisbech,
Cambridgeshire PE13 2BR Tel. 01945 466711
(supplier of a wide range of vegetable seed)

W. Robinson (Seeds and Plants) Ltd.,
Sunny Bank, Forton, Nr. Preston, Lancashire PR3 0BN
Tel: 01524 791210
(vegetable seeds and plants for the kitchen or show bench)

'Nemaslug'. www.nemasysinfo.com. Can be obtained from
The Green Gardener, 41 Strumpshaw Road, Brundall,
Norfolk. Tel. 01603 715096. www.greengardener.co.uk

Defenders Ltd, Occupation Road, Wye, Ashford, Kent. Tel. 01233 813121 www.defenders.co.uk (biological controls)

## Hedging suppliers

Buckingham Nurseries, Tingewick Road, Buckingham, MK18 4AE. Tel 01280 822133 www.hedging.co.uk (native hedging, trees, etc.)

Aveland Trees, Dunsby, Bourne, Linconshire PE10 0UB Tel. 01778 440716 (Locally sourced native hedging)

Fenleigh Willow, Broad Drove, Gosberton Clough, Spalding, Lincolnshire PE11 4JS. Tel. 01775 750478. (willow suitable for windbreaks)

## Organic Organisations

H.D.R.A., Ryton Organic Gardens, Ryton-on-Dunsmore, Coventry CV8 3LG Tel. 024 76303517 www.hdra.org.uk

Heritage Seed Library (address as above)
Members of HSL receive a choice of heritage/heirloom varieties of vegetable seeds each year.

The Soil Association, Bristol House, 40-56 Victoria Street, Bristol BS1 6BY Tel. 0117 9290661 www.soilassociation.org.

NOTES

NOTES